HOW TO GET ANYTHING YOU WANT? MAKE A MAGICK MIRROR!

MIKE NACH

Copyright © 2014 Mike Nach

All rights reserved.

ISBN-13: 978-1502765512

ISBN-10: 1502765519

TABLE OF CONTENTS

DISCLAIMER 1
INTRODUCTION 3
THE MAGICK MIRROR 7
BURNING DESIRE 13
THE MANIFESTATION PRINCIPLES 17
PREPARATORY EXERCISES 23
THE ART OF RELAXATION 27
THE QABALISTIC CROSS (QC) 31
THE CIRCUIT OF LIGHT (CL) EXERCISE 35
MAGICKAL VISUALIZATION 39
THE SECRET MANIFESTATION TECHNIQUE! 45
FAQ's ABOUT MAGICK MIRRORS 47
CONSTRUCTING A MAGICK MIRROR 51

   1: Metallic Universal Collector Mirror 51
   2: Organic Universal Collector Mirror 53

CHARGING A MAGICK MIRROR 57
USING THE MAGICK MIRROR 59

   I: How to use the magick mirror for manifestation of physical objects? 60
   II: How to use the magick mirror to attract money in your life? .. 63
   III: How to use the magick mirror to attract the person of your dreams? 65
   IV: How to use the magick mirror for healing? 67
   V: How to visit people or places, in the astral body, using the magick mirror? 69
   VI: How to use the magick mirror to time travel? 71
   VII: How to use the magick mirror to visit your parallel / alternate self in a parallel universe? 73
   VIII: How to use the magick mirror for exorcising 'possessed people' or 'haunted places'? 76

APPENDIX 79
   1: Tracing a Banishing Pentagram 79
   2: Planetary plants for organic fluid collector 81

Thank You! 83

MY OTHER BOOKS! 85

DISCLAIMER

The author and publisher have used their best efforts in preparing this book. Every effort has been made to accurately represent the product / techniques mentioned in this book, and their potential. Your level of success in attaining the results claimed in this book depends on the correctness of the construction of the product, precautions followed and the time you devote to the techniques, program and ideas given.

Since these factors differ according to individuals, we cannot guarantee your success. Nor are we responsible for any of your actions. Consulting a competent professional is advisable.

The author and publisher shall in no event be held liable to any party for any direct, indirect, punitive, special, psychological, incidental or other consequential damages arising, directly or indirectly, from any use of this material, which is provided "as is", and without warranties.

If you wish to apply the ideas contained in this book, you're taking full responsibility for your action.

INTRODUCTION

This is a book of white magick. It is not a book of spells or incantations for conjuring spirits or demons. It contains potent manifestation secrets taught by Western masters and Himalayan gurus to a select few. These closely guarded techniques will help you manifest practically anything you desire. You will figure out how the universe works, and how you can use this knowledge to turn your dreams into reality. Your life will be changed forever!

I am sure you have read about the magick mirror in fairy tales and folklore. Remember 'Aladdin and his Magic Lamp', 'Snow White and the Seven Dwarfs' and 'Alice in Wonderland.' Apparently, these stories may seem absurd but nonetheless they are founded on truth.

During the medieval ages, when persecution of occult knowledge was at its peak, the practitioners of the day were forced to go underground with their knowledge. To avoid detection, their knowledge was modified into stories which were passed from one generation to the next, distorting the original theme so much that the essence of the secret knowledge was lost. Fortunately, we are living in an age where all these hidden secrets have started crawling out of the woodwork……..

The magick mirror is a psychic **3D printer**. With its help, you can manifest anything you need- money, love, cars, houses, luxury items, good health, astral / time / inter-dimensional travel, exorcise spirits among other things. I have just scratched the surface in this book. There is not a single thing, in this world, that you cannot do with the use of the magick mirror. It is up to you to uncover the awesome powers of the magick mirror.

In addition to mirror magick, this book contains details of relaxation exercises; visualization and magickal exercises which will protect / strengthen / charge your inner energy system and develop your psychic powers.

Has the **Law of Attraction (LOA)** worked for you? No? The main reason why the LOA has not worked for most people is because they have apparently not been applying the Law of Attraction in the correct way. Anything half baked is doomed to fail. Does this make any sense? No? Let me help you. You and I will dine at a virtual restaurant where you will figure out what LOA and manifestation is really about. I will also be revealing **three startling secrets** about the universe which most LOA experts have failed to reveal in their teachings. These secrets are very essential for successful and long-lasting results. Intrigued? Read **THE MANIFESTATION PRINCIPLES**.

Some readers of the earlier edition of this book asked me whether it is possible to do manifestation without constructing a magick mirror. I can help you there. It is possible to manifest anything we desire without the help of a magick mirror. The chapter **THE SECRET MANIFESTATION TECHNIQUE!** will show you how. It is a six weeks program which you need to follow diligently. If you want easy, sure-fire techniques, then you will not find it here. Sorry! But, if you seriously practice my techniques, you will surely become a very successful manifestation wizard! Some of you will literally be plucking things out of thin air just like the Eastern mystics.

This revised edition is more understandable and more usable than the earlier edition. I request you to read it, page by page; study each concept and practice all the techniques given in this book, seriously.

There is nothing contrary to your moral, spiritual, religious or ethical values in this book. If you are looking for black magick or other harmful practices, then you will not find it here. Magick is meant to be used for the good of mankind!

Practice daily and diligently. If you are serious about making a massive, positive difference in your life, and committed to doing whatever it takes to make it happen then-

YOU WILL BECOME THE MASTER OF YOUR UNIVERSE!

THE MAGICK MIRROR

Have you often wondered what it would be like to be Aladdin and have his lamp with the powerful genie granting all your wishes? Is it wishful thinking? Apparently, not! It is possible to have such a device which will help you get anything you want in life. Of course, not as instantaneously as in Aladdin's tale but in the shortest time possible. This device is called the **'magick mirror'**.

A magick mirror is one of the most powerful occult tools known to man. If you are a geek, then you can call the magick mirror **a psychic 3D printer**. It is a device which can store or discharge, at the will of its user, any influence put into it. It will help the user to manifest any object of his desire-money, cars, house, love etc; perform psychic healing; visit people or places in the astral body and exorcise unwanted psychic entities from afflicted people or places. The list is endless. It will take time and lots of patience before you will become proficient with the effective usage of the magick mirror, but the results will be awesome.

The magick mirror is a genuine occult transmitter / receiver of universal forces. Once the mirror is charged with these forces, it automatically brings about very startling results for the user. In order to charge a magick mirror, a substance known as the 'fluid collector' is used for holding a charge into the mirror via the imagination of the user. Basic charging is done with a force called the **'akashic fluid'**.

The exact composition of this akashic fluid is not known since its existence has not been proved by pure science. According to the ancients, the akashic fluid permeates the entire universe and that matter is created from it. This fluid is very real and is the strongest and nicest fluid to work with. If an observer sits in front of a magick mirror properly charged with the akashic fluid, he will get the strange sensation of being very tiny and alone in the vastness of our universe.

According to physicists, we live in a multidimensional universe. Ancients, too, believed that our world is but a part of many other worlds which exist, alongside our physical world, in a different channel or wavelength. Each of these worlds is populated by beings with their own set of laws. Some physicists also believe that there are multi dimensional parallel universes where mirror images of us live in these dimensions. Occultists called these different wavelengths / dimensions as **'channels'** or **'planes'**. An analogy would be of a television set. The television set is the universe and we are one of the channels received by the set. Different planes occupy the same physical space in which we exist, but these planes are of different wavelengths not perceived by our eyes or instruments and so remain hidden from us. However, it is possible for us to visit these dimensions or summon the beings from these planes to our worlds, to communicate with them or do our bidding. This is the basis of black magick.

We, too, have three different planes within ourselves- **the physical, astral and mental planes of existence**. Astral planes are what have been described above. Mental plane is what is guided by our mind like visualization, our thoughts etc. Physical plane is our material plane of existence.

'Fluid' is another term frequently used in this book. It is a word used to describe the forces / fields pervading our universe. We all know that a fluid has the property of filling any container in which it is poured. Similarly, the energy fluid also fills the magick mirror in which it is 'poured' / 'charged'.

There are many types of psychic fluids pervading the different planes of our universe. Based on their psychic properties they are named 'elemental' fluids, 'light' fluids, 'electric' fluids, 'air/earth element' fluids, 'electro-magnetic' fluids and finally the 'akashic fluid'.

In this book, we are going to deal with the akashic fluid. This is the most powerful amongst the aforementioned fluids. An akashic fluid is similar to white light. White light is a mixture of all the colors of the rainbow. Likewise, the akashic fluid contains within it the essence of the above fluids.

A **'fluid collector'** is similar to an electric capacitor which has the capacity to hold an electric charge stored into it, until it is discharged. A fluid collector is also able to hold the fluids stored into it until they are discharged. The amount of fluids held by a fluid collector does not depend upon its mass or volume. A miniscule amount of these collectors are able to store a huge amount of a fluid. Our physical laws of space and size are not applicable to these psychic fluids.

Gold is one of the best collectors known. An atom of gold added to any collector greatly enhances the holding power of that compound, so a little gold must be added to all fluid collectors made. To add gold to a solid collector a tiny piece of gold or gold dust is simply put in the mixture.

Since gold has become so expensive we can add two to three drops of our blood to the collectors instead of gold. The user of the magick mirror will have to use his own blood which will bond him with the mirror.

Blood is equally effective as gold. Let me reiterate, that using a few drops of your own blood is not black magick.

Note: Remember, fluid collectors are not limited to just magick mirrors. You can use the collectors with any occult instrument or experiment to enhance its effect.

A magick mirror is usually concave in shape. It is observed that the flow of energy from the surface of the mirror leaves the mirror at an angle of ninety degrees to the surface and travels in straight lines. If a mirror is flat then the resultant flow of energy forms a column with parallel sides. Thus, if a concave mirror is used, then the energy will flow at right angles from every point on the mirrors surface forming a wide-angled energy field.

A word of caution: A magick mirror can also be used for harmful purposes. This falls in the realm of ritual or black magic and I am not in favor of it.

HOW THE UNIVERSE FULFILLS YOUR WISH

You input your wish with a clear visualized image.

The akashic fluid acts like a software and conveys your wish to the universe.

The universe acts like a processor and acts upon the instructions, given by the akashic fluid, to manifest your wish.

YOUR WISH COMES TRUE!

BURNING DESIRE

Ever pondered why some people are successful, while others not?

Successful people have well-defined goals and an intense burning desire for achieving it. Such people are often called "driven people." When you have a burning desire for a specific goal, you have strong emotions about it. Your conscious and subconscious minds are in harmony with each other. This heightened emotional response helps you overcome any obstacles while moving towards what you want to achieve.

Unsuccessful people, on the other hand, often focus on what other people have, instead of desiring what they really want. If you are crying out loud, "Hey! I am not like that!" then you are, probably, kidding yourself. The human mind thinks from a position of deficiency. It constantly thinks about what it did not get, what it does not have and why it needs that particular thing. So, consider very deeply whether you really need that wish to manifest in your life. Sometimes, what seems to be a very desirable thing, at the time, turns out to be decidedly less than desirable once it becomes a reality. Let your heart tell you what you need, not your mind!

Figure out whether your present 'desire' is a genuine desire or just a competitive wish to be one up over others. For example, your friend buys a new car and you immediately feel that you, too, need a similar car or one more expensive. You see images of expensive beautiful homes / luxury items and you believe you must have it because you want to be noticed.

Let us start out with a notebook or journal. At the top of the page, write what you truly need to manifest in your life. It could be money, material possessions, soul mate, health, anything. Define exactly what you want.

Let us consider some examples of goal setting- Do you need money? Write the exact amount down. Be specific about how you would like to receive it. Do not dream of a billion dollars at the first try. Your inner mind will not accept it due to past programming. Start with small amounts. After you succeed and gain confidence, then go after bigger cash piles. You can achieve anything, if your heart thinks you can!

Want a car? Which model? New or secondhand? Color? Features? If you know exactly which model you would like, get pictures of that model. Visualize it in your mind's eye. Clearly write down the features you would like in this new car and the reasons why you desire it.

Remember, if you are not specific about your wish then the universe will not know how to fulfill it. That's it!

Ask yourself these questions-

- Is this what I truly (heartfelt) desire?

- Why I want it?

- Will it really benefit me and make me happy?

- Is there any aspect in this goal I want, based on a past experience?

If you have any thoughts you have on the above questions, write them below your goal. Let your ideas flow and write whatever comes to mind. It is necessary to decide and know beyond any doubt that you really need the object of your desire and that your life will be enhanced by it in a positive way.

Do not take immediate action on what you have written. Read it for a couple of days and ponder over it. Make changes. Very soon, you will have a clear picture of your true desire.

Do not tell anyone about your goals. The minute you start telling others, the energy that you have build up is gone.

Develop a blueprint with strategies for achieving your goal. Be focused on one goal at a time. You cannot take action in multiple directions at once. It is strenuous and non-productive. Let every part of your mind, body and soul be filled with your burning desire.

Believe it can happen! This is when the universe will help you out.

THE MANIFESTATION PRINCIPLES

Did you ever try to manifest something you desire and found it hard to make it possible? Are you going to holler, "This LOA stuff is B.S"? Before you do that, check out the manifestation methods followed by you. Perhaps, you were not going about it the correct way?

Let us go to a fancy restaurant. There, you will figure out what the universal laws of manifestation are truly about and how to use them for your benefit.

1: The universe is like a fancy dining restaurant.

2: Do you go in and order, "Give me some food?" Is the waiting staff supposed to figure out what you want? So, what's going to happen? Patrons will stare at you. They are going to think you are crazy! The server might reluctantly hand you a menu card and ask what you would like to order. Most likely, they will ignore you and you will remain hungry.

3: The same rule applies to our goals and desires. Goals like, "I need a new car," or "I need a new love in my life," or "I need lots of money," are not specific. Define exactly what you want. Just as you would order in a restaurant, the universe requires precise orders from you. If your orders are vague then you might end up receiving nothing or something you do not want.

4: After ordering, are you going to doubt whether the food will arrive at your table? I am sure you wouldn't! Similarly, be confident while ordering from the universe and be sure that you will receive what you have precisely ordered. Believe! If you are negative, the results will be likewise. Your wishes (positive or negative) will manifest just as you asked for. That's **Law of Attraction** for you!

5: If you reject what the universe offers you (based on your vague request), the universe is going to conclude that you are unreasonable, ungrateful and difficult to please. It will stop granting your future wishes. Then, please do not complain, "The universe sucks!"

6: Do you expect the waiting staff to instantly serve your order? It takes a while for the wait staff to take your order and submit it to the kitchen. The kitchen staff then prepares the dishes you have ordered. The universe works at its own speed. It chooses the right environmental conditions while granting your wish. Do not expect immediate results. Some wishes may take a longer time to manifest. Be patient and you will be amply rewarded.

7: What happens if you place an order and then when it arrives, you do not like it? Do you eat it or send it back? Make a scene? Post negative reviews online? What if the universe brought you what you wanted but it wasn't what you really wanted? Throw a fit? Don't! Instead, open your mind to accept what the universe has offered you. If you do this, you will find the universe has fulfilled your wish in a different way then you originally thought of. In retrospect, you will realize that this was best for you. So, do not cry out aloud if you receive something different.

8: What would happen if you kept on changing your order frequently at the restaurant before it arrived? Is the wait staff going to be happy with your indecisive behavior? No way! They might not serve you or you will be disappointed with the poor service. Likewise, do not screw up your orders with the universe, by frequently changing it. What's your problem? Why are you not clear about what you want? If you are going to be a jerk, then the universe will treat you like one.

9: If you have read any of **"The Law of Attraction (LOA)"** books, there are **three startling aspects** about the Universe which the LOA experts have overlooked in their teachings. You need to follow these rules in order to be truly successful in your manifestation endeavors.

They are-

i. "There ain't no such thing as a free lunch" (TANSTAAFL). Don't we ask for the check (bill) after eating in a restaurant? Believe it or not! The universe expects payment for fulfilling our wishes! Startled?

Our universe is a giving universe. It will give you whatever you ask. However, you need to constantly give in order to constantly receive from it. If you ignore this rule, the universe will force you to give back in some unhappy way. Have you ever wondered why some people who are apparently successful (lottery or jackpot winners, pop stars, inheritors) but have relationship, health and other problems? Perhaps they have not paid the universal bill!

This **"paying the universe"** secret was known and practiced by the ancient Egyptians, Greeks, Jews, Romans, Indians and the Chinese. The modern rich, too, have used philanthropy to give back to society what they have received. So, shouldn't you?

Unlike a restaurant's check, the universe has no set price for any wish granted by it. You set the price and the time period for making the payment. While asking the universe to fulfill your wish, promise it that you will pay the tab (you decide how much), within a specified time period, after your wish is fulfilled. Remit this amount to your church or any other religious or charitable organization. Paying relatives or friends does not count. Do so freely and joyously. You will be able to enjoy what the universe has bestowed you.

ii. "There ain't no lunch during closing hours" (TANLDCH)
Each restaurant has its fixed opening (business) hours as well as closing hours. If you saunter in a restaurant near its closing time, expect to see the wait staff's surly faces and poor service. Is it also possible to enter a restaurant during its closing hours and expect to be served food? I bet, not! They will not let you in.

The ancients believed that there were certain time periods in a day when the universe is either responsive or totally unresponsive to your wish pleas. If you ask the universe during the **"positive"** period, it speeds up the manifestation process. If you try coaxing the universe during the **"negative"** period, it simply will not budge. The time period between the "positive" and the "negative" periods is the **"average"** period. Figure out what that means!

These periods vary from place to place. No worry. It is according to the local time, at the place, where you live. No calculations or conversions of EDT, PST or GMT involved.

Why not give it a try? Try to ask the universe during the "positive" periods for quick service. Abstain during the "negative" periods. Check out the table on the next page.

DAY	HOURS	
	POSITIVE	NEGATIVE
SUNDAY	15.00-16.30	16.30-18.00
MONDAY	13.30-15.00	7.30-9.00
TUESDAY	12.00-13.30	15.00-16.30
WEDNESDAY	10.30-12.00	12.00-13.30
THURSDAY	9.00-10.30	13.30-15.00
FRIDAY	7.30-9.00	10.30-12.00
SATURDAY	6.00-7.30	9.00-10.30

iii. "Familiarity breeds good service! (FBGS)" If you are a regular customer of any restaurant, you will definitely get special treatment from the restaurant staff. Similarly, try to be a "regular customer" of the universe. Talk to it whenever you can (not loudly, otherwise people may think you are crazy). Thank it for being your friend and for fulfilling your wishes. Respect, believe and obey the rules of the universe. The universe will start giving you preferential treatment. Believe me!

10: Finally, Don't we all tip the wait staff while paying the check? The universe, too, expects a tip from us after it has fulfilled our order. **Gratitude and Thanks!** Remember to be grateful and thankful after your wish is fulfilled. The universe expects and appreciates that!

That's it, people! The next time you visit an earthly restaurant or deal with the universal restaurant, remember what I have said above.

PREPARATORY EXERCISES

Everything in this universe is made of energy. All of us are energy sources constantly radiating energy out in space. This type of energy varies from individual to individual and depends upon the physical, mental, emotional and spiritual state of the person. It is known by various names- **aura, vibes or prana**. This energy field is three dimensional and surrounds our physical body in all directions. If we have a strong energy field then we have balanced health - **physical, mental, emotional and spiritual**. Our energy system gets depleted when we are sick, stressed, depressed, in pain or if people around us irritate us or suck our energies. Being around negative people, visiting haunted places or cemeteries, smoking, taking drugs and alcohol also saps our energy! Having healthy habits helps a lot in maintaining our inner energy!

Did you ever wonder why a happy person radiates a "glow" which inspires happiness in those around them and, by the same token, spending time with a "negative vibes" person seems to drain you of your energy? A person having positive vibes will always attract good things to them and a negative person just the opposite!

Ever tinkered with a magnet? I am sure you have. What's a magnet? Why is one steel bar a magnet and the other not? The answer lies in their molecular arrangement. (See below) An ordinary steel bar has molecules scattered in various directions within it. If these molecules are made to align in the same direction then the steel bar gets magnetized and attracts other magnetic substances towards it. However, if you heat or start battering a magnet, the molecules lose their alignment and the magnet ceases to be a magnet.

Arrangement of molecules

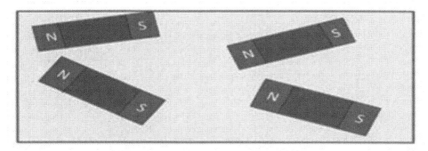

Unmagnetized Bar

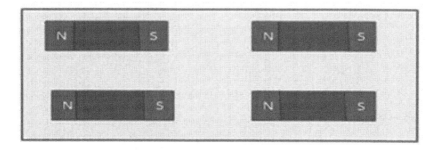

Magnetized Bar

So, how do we become a manifestation magnet?

It is a scientific fact that all energy vibrates. Since we are energy sources, we, too, vibrate and so does everything else. According to the Law of Attraction, "Like Attracts Like." Therefore, like vibrations will also attract one another. It also means that to get or achieve something, you will need to match yourself with its vibration. To manifest your wishes into your life, you have to **align your vibrations** with your desire. It is impossible for a person whose mind is absorbed with negative thoughts of scarcity and fear to do this. Such a person will always remain unmagnetized!

Luckily, there are techniques which can turn an unmagnetized person into a manifestation magnet. How do we go about it?

We start by learning to relax and being in a proper frame of mind, called the 'alpha state,' with **the Relaxation Exercise**. Then we must practice the two magickal exercises- **"The Qabalistic Exercise"** and **"The Circuit of Light Exercise"** which will align / replenish the energy fields and empower us. These exercises will also awaken the higher faculties of perception within us, which are so essential for successful manifestation.

THE ART OF RELAXATION

We all know that we will not have the desired result if we are tense. These tensions need to be released. Our conscious mind turns highly negative when we are not relaxed. We lose contact with our subconscious mind. We are skeptical of the possibility of our wishes coming true.

The magick mirror is a psychic generator / amplifier. If we are in a negative state of mind, while using the mirror, we might not get any results or worse our negative thoughts might come true.

When we relax, we become more receptive. Our conscious mind and subconscious mind are in harmony with each other. We become energized. Our wishes get fulfilled!

We need to reach a relaxed state of mind called the **'alpha state'** before we try to manifest anything. It is in this state that miracles happen, which is otherwise not possible when we are in the normal state. The alpha state is the first state beyond normal waking beta state and occurs when our brainwaves reach 8-12 cycles per second of activity. If you already know techniques for entering the alpha state then use them. There are various methods for inducing the mind to the alpha state such as Silva mind control, mp3 relaxation tapes, the Morry method etc. Use any method which will help you.

I am introducing the following two methods that have worked for me. Check out which method suits you.

Technique # 1

1: Sit in the room where you will be conducting the mirror magick / manifestation exercise. It also helps if you will practice the relaxation exercise sitting on the same chair which you will be using during the actual mirror / manifestation experiment. Your mind will start associating that chair with relaxation and you will be in a relaxed state quicker.

2: Start with taking a long deep breath and holding it for a few seconds. Then exhale this breath and allow your eyes to close. Do this a few times. Let go of the surface tension in your body.

3: Now, become aware of your eye muscles and relax the muscles around your eyes completely. Hold onto that relaxation until the muscles of the eyes are not able to move and test them to make sure they are not moving.

4: Now, you can have the same quality of relaxation throughout your whole body as the relaxation you are experiencing in your eyes. Just let this quality of relaxation flow through your whole body from the top of your head to the tips of your toes.

5: We can deepen this relaxation even more. Begin by opening and closing your eyes. When you close your eyes, it is your signal that this feeling of relaxation is becoming 10 times deeper.

6: Now, open your eyes / now close your eyes and feel that relaxation flowing through your entire body, taking you much deeper. Imagine that your whole body is covered and wrapped in a warm cocoon of relaxation.

7: Repeat the above procedure one more time and double your relaxation.

8: And now, open your eyes and figure out how you felt before / during and after this exercise.

Do you feel more, or less relaxed than before? If yes, then you are in the alpha state and are ready for magick. Always perform this relaxation exercise before you start your occult operations / using the magick mirror.

Technique # 2

This is a very easy technique. I use it whenever I want to calm myself instantaneously.

1: Sit in the room where you will be conducting the mirror magick / manifestation exercise. It also helps if you will practice the relaxation exercise sitting on the same chair which you will be using during the actual mirror / manifestation experiment. Your mind will start associating that chair with relaxation and you will be in a relaxed state quicker.

2: Start by taking a long deep breath.

3: Exhale this breath after holding it for a few seconds. Do this a few times.

4: Let go of the surface tension in your body.

5: With your eyes closed, direct your gaze to a spot between your eyebrows.

6: Touch the tip of your tongue to the roof of your mouth.

7: Sit in this position for a while and feel the deep sense of calm engulfing you.

That's it! You have entered the alpha state.

Open your eyes and figure out how you felt before / during and after you performed the above exercise. Do you feel a perceptible change?

THE QABALISTIC CROSS (QC)

Though this ritual looks simple, it is a potent tool for self-development. If you do the **QC** daily, you will soon find a change in yourself. People around You will notice that you are looking more radiant, confident and successful. Your energy system will be aligned. Just focus on the ritual and not the result. The results will come automatically if you stay focused and believe in the powers of this ritual. So, Let us try it out.

1: Stand in the middle of a quiet room and face east.

2: Take deep breaths and let go of the surface tension in your body.

3: With your eyes closed, direct your gaze to a spot between your eyebrows.

4: Touch the tip of your tongue to the roof of your mouth.

5: Stand in this position for a while and feel the deep sense of calm engulfing you.

6: Now visualize a bright sphere of light above your head.

7: Keep your left hand at your side and make a fist of your right hand and point with the extended forefinger at this sphere and bring it down to your forehead. Visualize that you are bringing this light from above and filling your head with its powerful and positive energy. While doing so vibrate (saying in a sonorous voice)

YOU ARE

8: Bring your finger to the center of your chest and imagine the light from your head is flowing through your chest and straight into the ground. While doing so, vibrate

THE KINGDOM

9: Now, touch your right shoulder. As you do this, visualize a beam of light originating from your chest and extending past your right shoulder. Focus on this horizontal beam of light and vibrate

AND THE POWER

10: Touch your left shoulder and visualize the beam of light now extending from your chest outwards past your left shoulder. As you focus on this light, vibrate

AND THE GLORY

11: Clasp your hands over your chest as if praying and vibrate

FOREVER, AMEN

12: At this point, you should visualize yourself as a being of awesome light and energy, shining in all directions. Stand in this position as long as you want. You have become part of a giant cross of positive light flowing through you.

Note: First thing in the morning and the last thing before going to bed is the best time to do the QC. If it is possible, do it twice a day. Practice this on a regular basis. If you are inconsistent, the results will be likewise. Make it a daily habit. The QC may also be performed before and after any meditative / mirror magick / occult operation. It helps to protect and charge your energy system. I recommend this exercise strongly as it awakens the latent powers within us, helping us to achieve our goals.

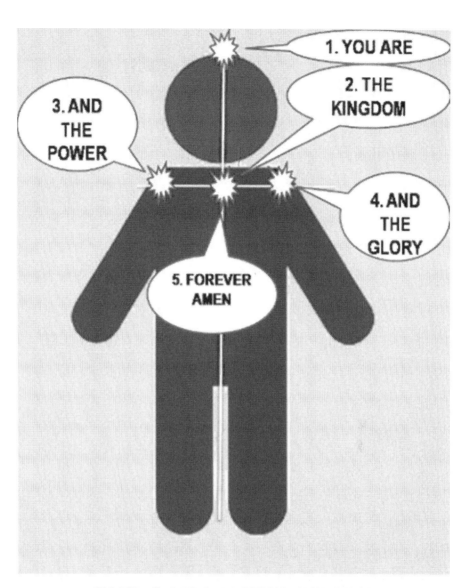

THE QABALISTIC CROSS

THE CIRCUIT OF LIGHT (CL) EXERCISE

This is another simple, yet powerful exercise which will awaken your spiritual energies and higher faculties of perception. If you do this ritual daily, you will activate your **'PSYCHIC VISION'** faculties. You will be able to visualize things beyond your normal senses. This faculty is required if you wish to use the magick mirror to time travel and to visit people / places and parallel universes / dimensions in your astral form. Try out this exercise as follows:

1: Sit in the room where you will be conducting the mirror magick / manifestation exercise. It also helps if you will practice the relaxation exercise sitting on the same chair which you will be using during the actual mirror / manifestation experiment. Your mind will start associating that chair with relaxation and you will be in a relaxed state quicker.

2: Take deep breaths and perform the relaxation exercise.

3: Remain in the relaxed state for a while and feel the deep sense of calm engulfing you.

4: Now, visualize a bright sphere of light on the crown (top) of your head (**crown center**). Hold on to this position for a while. At the start, you might not be able to visualize anything. With constant practice, you will be successful. So, keep at it.

5: Now, slowly imagine a band of light from the crown center traveling to the area between your eyes (**brow center**) and forming another ball of white light. Hold on to this position for a while.

6: Now, let a band of light flow from the brow center to the throat area (**throat center**) and imagine it forming a ball of white light there. Hold on to this position for a while.

7: Now, draw a band of light from your throat center to your heart area (**heart center**) and imagine it forming a ball of white light there. Hold on to this position for a while.

8: Finally, complete the circuit by drawing a band of light from the heart center and connecting it to your crown center.

9: Repeat steps 4 to 8, two to three times.

10: After you have done this, breathe deeply and circulate this bright band of light from the crown center - brow center - throat center - heart center - crown center continuously for a few minutes.

11: Open your eyes and imagine how you felt before / during and after you performed the above exercise. Do you feel a perceptible change?

12: Try out this exercise atleast once a day, if possible. It will help you develop your psychic powers.

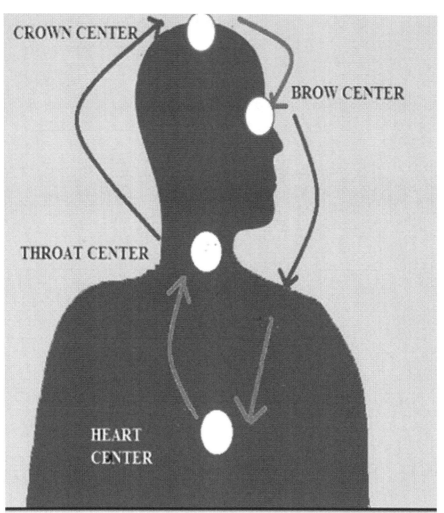

THE CIRCUIT OF LIGHT (CL) EXERCISE

MAGICKAL VISUALIZATION

The basic theory of the **Law of Attraction** goes like this- *"If you want something, you put your mind to have it, and then you **visualize** and feel it as if it is something you already have. Do that consistently and take appropriate action. When you do this, you will attract that thing in your life."*

That's right! **Visualization** is the key to successful manifestation. If you have read about successful men and women in history, they have all used visualization techniques to be successful. Mirror magick and manifestation techniques need visualization to work.

Before I discuss visualization, let me emphasize- **daydreaming** is not visualization. Daydreaming is automatic. During daydreaming, your unconscious mind does whatever it wants. It rarely involves your other senses. Daydreams are most often inconsistent. A daydreaming scenario hardly lasts for long in your head. They are fleeting images. You could call it **wishful thinking**. When you add conscious act to your daydream, it becomes closer to visualization. Visualization should have a firm structure and intention. You need to fully concentrate during the visualization process and also include all five senses to the pictured image, one by one, and to really see yourself in the image you have created.

When you visualize, you have an intention behind it. You create an energy field (vibrations) with this intention. And, if you made use of all your senses while visualizing, then the vibrations of your visualized image will align with the vibrations of the desired object. What happens then? Voila! Your visualized image becomes a reality!

How do you get there?

As I've said above, visualization means not only seeing, but hearing, smelling and feeling the object of our desire (using your senses). If you visualize a rose then you should be able to see it clearly in your mind's eye; feel the petals / thorns; smell the fragrance of the flower. This image should be so vivid as to appear real.

Are you able to do this? I couldn't when I first tried it out. It took me six weeks to master this technique. After that, visualization was a cinch. You need to practice consistently for **atleast six weeks** before you become comfortable with the manifestation procedures. I am sorry but there are no quick-fire techniques here. Be patient and practice diligently. You will be awesomely successful. Shall we begin?

Let us start-

Set aside 30-60 minutes every day for visualization practice.

Go to the special place where you have been practicing the relaxation and the magickal exercises. Sit in a comfortable position and do the relaxation exercise and the Qabalistic Cross. These exercises should be performed whenever you carry put your visualization exercises.

First week:

Keep a simple two dimensional drawing / picture in front of you. Study this for one-two minutes and then close your eyes. Try forming a mental image of it. If the image is not clear, open your eyes and compare the real picture against any part of your mental picture. Figure out the imperfections. Close your eyes and form a clearer image again. You will need to practice this for a week till you master it.

Second week:

If you are able to perform the above exercise without difficulty then graduate to three dimensional objects. Your goal should be to form a mental image exactly like the original. Try examining the visualized objects from various angles-above, below, etc. Start with smaller objects at first like your cell phone, pen, watch or anything else that takes your fancy. Once you are able to visualize smaller objects clearly, go for larger objects. After you are able to do this, try reducing this "large" image to fit it between your cupped hands.

Third week:

The next step is visualizing color. Find six pieces of paper, fabric of the following colors-red, blue, yellow, green, white and dark violet. *(The Decimal code for dark violet is R=148, G=0, B=211)* Choose any three of the above colors per day. Stay with a particular color until you can instantly recollect that color. Start by looking intently at the paper or fabric of a particular color. Flood your mind with the chosen color. After you are able to see the color vividly in your mind, then try this with another color. Practice this for three to four days. After this, test your color formation skills for the remaining days of the week. Work on the dark violet color. Are you able to see it clearly in your mind's eye? This particular color is very important because It is the color of the akashic fluid.

Fourth week:

Activate your audition (hearing), gustation (taste), olfactory (smell) and tactile (touch) senses- Visualize your favorite food item and feel the taste; Visualize your partner by your side and smell his / her fragrance; Imagine you are at a music concert and hear your favorite band playing. Your visualized images should look, feel, smell, hear and taste (optional) real.

Fifth week:

So far, our image building was locked up inside our minds. True magickal visualization requires the chosen image to be "projected" into the real world.

Close your eyes and visualize a three dimensional object. Now slowly open your eyes while still retaining your mental image in all its details. You should be able to "see" the mental image just as if it were a natural part of your surroundings. Initially start with small objects and then when you get confident, go bigger. Give it your full attention. These images should appear "real." If the image fades, take a break and repeat the procedure. Continue in this way until you are able to hold this projected image in front of you for atleast thirty seconds.

Sixth week:

You will try to form the akashic cloud between your hands. Close your eyes and form a dark violet cloud in your mind's eye. Cup your hands in front of you and slowly open your eyes retaining the image of this violet cloud. Project this cloud between your hands. Are you able to feel it? Hold this image for as long as you are able. If it fades repeat the whole procedure again. Practice till you get it right.

Okay, folks! Don't groan, "OMG! Do I need to go through this grind to become a manifestation wizard? The techniques taught in other LOA books are so much easier!" Well! Go ahead and follow those techniques. If they work for you, then it is fine by me. But, if you want to be a true manifestation wizard, who dreams of plucking out objects from thin air, then you need to put in some effort. The results will be awesome!

Remember this. There's a **danger** zone, too. Learn to control your powers of visualization. Do not allow these images to control you. You should not allow any image to form in front of you when you don't want it. Also, don't be obsessed with creating visual images all the time. This might lead to **involuntary hallucinations**.

THE SECRET MANIFESTATION TECHNIQUE!

I have had readers of the previous editions of this book telling me that constructing the magick mirror is beyond them. Is there a way to experience a magick mirror's powers without making one? Yes! There is! It is possible to manifest anything we desire without the help of a magick mirror.

I will teach you a secret and powerful technique taught by Western masters and Himalayan gurus to a select few, until now. With years of daily practice, they were able to instantaneously manifest objects out of thin air. If you seriously practice this technique, you will be like them (be patient).

This technique uses the powers of the akashic fluid to manifest anything we desire. The akashic fluid is the basis of all creation (matter). Every form or process in nature is the visible expression of this akashic fluid. It is an intelligent substance. It is capable of taking any form and solidifying it to create matter. The akashic fluid understands the language of pictures rather than words. It acts as the software of the Universal 3D Printer. Hence, visualization plays an important role in the manifestation process. If we are able to pictorially impress our desire upon the akashic fluid, it would start to create that thing for us, along with a situation / opportunity for making it a reality. In other words, whatever we desire will not appear out of thin air, instantaneously. It will, however, appear in our life miraculously within a reasonable time period. We need to keep our eyes open to recognize it, when it comes, and take possession of it.

Based on this theory, we shall use the powers of visualization / akashic fluid to create whatever we want in life. The equation for manifestation is as follows:

VISUALIZATION + AKASHIC FLUID = SUCCESSFUL MANIFESTATION

In the earlier chapters, you have learnt the art of relaxation and visualization. If you have seriously practiced these exercises then you should be able to project an image of any object in front of you. You should also be able to create a vivid image of a dark violet cloud between your cupped hands. If you are ready, then it is time to perform the manifestation exercise.

1: Go to the special place where you have been practicing the relaxation and the magickal exercises. Sit in a comfortable position and do the Qabalistic Cross and the relaxation exercise.

2: Visualize a dark violet cloud between your slightly cupped hands. Think of it as the akashic fluid. Impregnate this cloud with a clear and specific image of the object of your desire (car, house, money, partner, dream on). Please do not fill the akashic fluid with multiple images at a time. You have to be focused in your desires, remember that. Do not jam the akashic fluid's circuits with multiple wishes at the same time.

3: Firmly, request the akashic fluid that you want this object to manifest in your life. Do not set any time period for wish fulfilment. Promise the akashic fluid that you will pay for the service. Do not break this promise.

4: Release this cloud containing the image of your desired object and let it float away to carry out your order. Have faith. If you have carried out this technique correctly, then your wish is definitely going to come true.

5: Always show your gratitude / express thanks to the astral fluid / universe after it has carried out your order.

Once you master this technique, you will be able to manifest anything you want.

FAQ's ABOUT MAGICK MIRRORS

I have received wonderful and also some brutally frank reviews (ouch!), from my readers, for the earlier edition of this book. I would like to thank them for their views and suggestions. This has motivated me to write a better book. I hope you will like this revised edition and I invite you to share your views with me.

These are my replies to some of the FAQs:

1: Construction of the magick mirror isn't easy-

I agree. The blueprint given in my earlier book was not easy to follow. The **magick mirrors** given in this book require very little expertise and the materials are easy to get.

2: Gold and Silver are prohibitively expensive-

Yes! Gold and Silver prices are reaching the stratosphere. Only one of the two mirrors described in this book has gold / silver as their components. The other mirror uses inexpensive organic materials.

3: Using drops of your blood is akin to black magic. Demons, monsters and other critters will be attracted to blood and come rushing out of the mirror-

I don't blame some of my readers for having this fear. Their unfounded fears are based on the movies they have seen and the books, internet stuff they may have read. The media has perverted an ancient process to suit their ends and make money.

For God's sake! I am just talking about a few drops of our own blood. There's no animal or human sacrifice involved.

Demons and other unworldly critters don't come rushing towards us when we take a few drops of blood. Heck! They are not sharks! If such a thing was possible, then every injured and bleeding person would have been attacked by these creatures.

Demons and other unworldly creatures need to be summoned by spells and sacrifices. Blood used in such rituals is sanctified and, thus, different from ordinary blood. Personally, I have used a few drops of blood while constructing my mirrors and never encountered any problems. Blood is one of the best collectors of akashic fluid known. It enhances the holding capacity of a magick mirror. It is a substitute for gold which has become very expensive.

However, if you still queasy about using blood then do not use it.

No demon or creepy crawly is ever going to come out of the mirror unless you open the doorways to their worlds and let them in.

4: Skepticism about the existence of the akashic fluid and its role in the manifestation process-

The akashic fluid is still an unknown concept in modern science. Scientists are confounded by "dark matter" and "dark energy." Many ancient concepts are being re-discovered by scientists. The akashic fluid will have to await its turn. No matter, the akashic fluid is very real. Believe in it! It exists! Use it! You will benefit greatly!

5: Charging, programming the mirror with akashic fluid sounds complicated-

Every new task seems complicated in the beginning. Skepticism also hinders our progress. If you persist and practice diligently you will realize that it is not that difficult.

Please do not expect results at the first try. Be patient and positive. C'mon guys! Some effort is necessary if you want to acquire something.

6: Can we manifest our wishes without using a magick mirror?

The basic advantage of a magick mirror is that it hastens the process of manifestation. Once you charge, load and programme a mirror with your wish, then it is on auto pilot. You don't need to repeat the process every day. Other non-mirror methods require repeated attempts and faith to accomplish our goals. For readers who do not wish to construct a magick mirror, I have described a very potent, non mirror, **manifestation exercise** which is equally effective. It is a method used by the masters in their manifestation miracles. If you master this technique then you will have great power in your hands!

7: Are there any dangers associated with astral travels and visiting other dimensions?

Astral and inter-dimensional traveling is actually a very pleasant experience. However, if you are unprepared for this experience then you might, initially, feel scared / bewildered.

You might encounter spirits of recently dead people who are trying to find their way. Yes! There are also negative and ignorant entities (elementals) in the astral realm. They cannot harm you as long as you are not afraid of them. You should ignore them, if they accost you, and show that you are in control. Such creatures feed on fear and when they sense an astral traveler's fears they surround him / her like a pack of hungry dogs.

So, if you are timid or having psychotic problems, then don't venture into astral / time or inter-dimensional traveling. It is not for you. Stay away!

8: Is it possible to use the magick mirror for dark magick, to evoke spirits, demons and other astral creatures?

Yes, you definitely can! However, I am totally against this category of magick and so would not like to discuss this topic further. As it is, there is a lot of evil in this world and I don't want to open more avenues for evil.

Have you ever wondered why demons and malevolent spirits roam our world? Practitioners of black magick invoke these out-worldly creatures to our world to do their bidding. There's an unwritten magickal rule that after the work is done, these creatures should be sent back to their worlds safely. A few black magicians disobey this rule, leaving these 'homeless' creatures to wander aimlessly in our world. Some of them are so pissed off that they start possessing humans / animals, attacking us or engaging in poltergeist activity. Be considerate!

9: What things are possible with the magick mirror?

There is not a single thing you cannot do with the use of the magick mirror. It is one of the most powerful occult devices known to man. This book describes some of the uses of the magick mirror.

Use your imagination for other uses. However, it requires a lot of patience and daily practice before you become proficient in mirror magick. Once, you reach that stage, you will literally become a creator of your own universe!

CONSTRUCTING A MAGICK MIRROR

In this chapter, we will discuss the construction of two types of magick mirrors:

1- Metallic universal collector mirror

2- Organic universal collector mirror

Both are equally powerful. So, check out which mirror will be easy to construct and suit your purpose.

1: Metallic Universal Collector Mirror

This type of mirror requires the various planetary metals including gold and silver which are expensive metals. This mirror will be effective for a very long period, unless damaged. If you can bear the cost, then go ahead.

Materials:

1: A shallow, concave shaped, clear glass / porcelain / China / earthenware / plastic plate or bowl, which should be six inches in diameter or more.

2: Ingredients for metallic collector: Tiny, equal parts [by size/volume] of gold / gold tincture (or two/three drops of your blood as a substitute for gold. Your choice.), silver, tin, mercury, copper, lead, iron, charcoal and ten parts of powdered quartz / powdered resin (or amber if available) mixed together.

3: Black acrylic or water soluble paint.

Construction:

1: Wash the bowl with salt water and then with fresh water. Dry it with a lint-free cloth.

2: Paint the inside part [the inside part is the part that would hold a liquid if it was poured in it] of the concave bowl with the black paint.

3: Sprinkle the metallic collector over the paint while it is still wet.

4: After this, apply several thin coats of paint over this until the surface appears smooth. Ensure that the previous coat is dry before applying the next one.

5: Do not touch the inner surface of the bowl before the paint has dried or your fingerprints will be plainly visible on the finished article.

Your metallic universal collector mirror is ready for use.

Precautions:

When not in use, wrap the mirror in a clean previously unused silk cloth to prevent any unwanted psychic influences from affecting the mirror.

Silk is one of the finest known insulators for occult forces and is used for keeping magickal instruments from getting contaminated by unwanted outside forces.

2: Organic Universal Collector Mirror

It is easier to prepare an organic universal collector mirror because the plant material, used, is easily available and inexpensive. Since the components are organic, the effectiveness of this mirror will diminish over a period of time. You will need to apply a fresh coat of the organic collector and paint periodically.

Materials:

1: A shallow, concave shaped, clear glass / porcelain / China / earthenware / plastic plate or bowl, which should be six inches in diameter or more.

2: Ingredients for organic collector: Equal and sufficient quantities of cypress leaves, bark or wood; bean root, leaves or seeds; rose leaves or flowers; nettle or oak leaves; clover leaves; bay leaves (laurel) or grape vine leaves; willow or ivy leaves; a few drops of almond oil. [For more varieties of planetary plants and preparation of the organic fluid collector, see **Appendix #2: Planetary plants for organic fluid collector**]

3: Two teaspoons of powdered quartz (optional).

4: A suitable food preservative.

5: Black acrylic or water soluble paint.

Construction:

1: Wash the bowl with salt water and then with fresh water. Dry it with a lint-free cloth.

2: Cut the above plants/herbs / roots into small pieces.

3: Add 5/8th cup of distilled water to the cut pieces and then grind them to a smooth paste.

4: Put a little quantity of food preservative to this paste and mix well.

5: Add two teaspoons of powdered quartz (optional) to the paste and mix well.

6: Paint the inside of the concave bowl with the black paint.

7: After the paint has dried, smear the organic paste evenly over the painted surface. Ensure that the inside of the bowl is completely covered with this paste. Allow it to dry.

8: After this, apply several thin coats of black paint over this until the surface appears smooth. Ensure that the previous coat is dry before applying the next one.

9: Do not touch the inner surface of the bowl before the paint has dried or your fingerprints will be plainly visible on the finished article.

Your organic universal collector mirror is ready for use.

Precautions:

When not in use, wrap the mirror in a clean previously unused silk cloth to prevent any unwanted psychic influences from affecting the mirror.

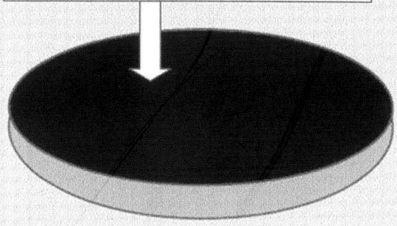

CHARGING A MAGICK MIRROR

You should try out mirror magick in a room where you will not be disturbed by loud noise and people. The windows, if any, should have dark curtains so that the room will be sufficiently dark but not that dark that you are not able to see the mirror placed before you on the table. You should have a table and chair in the room for carrying out the operation. Please ensure that the table has no glass or shiny top which will reflect light and distract you.

Charging the mirror is as follows:

1: Sit comfortably on a chair, in front of a table, in a semi darkened room. It is preferable to sit facing a blank wall or the dark curtains.

2: Remove the mirror from its silk cloth covering and place it near you on the table.

3: Make sure that there is enough light to see the mirror but ensure that no light is reflected directly in the mirror. This must be followed whenever you use the mirror.

4: Do the relaxation exercise.

5: Proceed to clear the mirror, of any previous charges present on it, as follows- Imagine that the surface of the mirror has turned black and that anything in this mirror is being sucked and absorbed into this blackness. Now dissolve the blackness complete with the impurities collected into the space around the mirror and visualize it becoming smaller and smaller vanishing into nothingness. The mirror will now be ready for charging.

6: Form a dark violet cloud between your cupped hands and direct it onto the surface of the magick mirror. The akashic fluid will be absorbed on coming in contact with the fluid collector of the mirror. Proceed to lock the charge and program it to carry out any task you have planned to be carried with the help of the mirror.

7: Locking the charge in the mirror is carried out by an act of will-power. As soon as the akashic fluid has been absorbed into the mirror's surface you should with all the will-power and optimism you can muster, state in your mind that the charge will remain there as long as you require it.

8: You can also charge a mirror in such a way that it recharges itself continuously so that its charge will never be emptied.

9: If you use the continuous charging method then do not wrap the mirror in silk cloth when it is in use, otherwise silk will block the charging. Keep such continuously charging mirrors in a safe place to prevent others from touching it and disturbing the charging process. If this happens, then you will have to clear the mirror and start the charging process all over again.

10: Programming the charge is slightly a difficult procedure which can be accomplished after some practice. You must state in your mind that the charge which has been locked into the mirror will start flowing from the mirror either at this instant or at a pre-determined time, rate and period.

The mirror is now ready to accomplish any task fed into it.

USING THE MAGICK MIRROR

Using the magick mirror will speed up your manifestation efforts. There's not a single thing that you cannot do with the use of the magick mirror. It works! However, you need to prepare yourself and practice a lot before you become proficient in mirror magick. I would like to again remind you not to expect perfect results at the first try. Try, try and you will succeed. Lots of patience is necessary for success. The results will be awesome!

Please read the chapters (**THE MANIFESTATION PRINCIPLES** and **FAQ's ABOUT MAGICK MIRRORS**) before you use the mirror. Some operations like astral and inter-dimensional traveling may not be suitable for some people. If you feel uneasy then, please, do not attempt further.

Let us discuss some of the uses of a magick mirror.

I: How to use the magick mirror for manifestation of physical objects?

It is advisable that initially you should start small like small amounts of cash, appliances, mobile devices etc. As your powers of focus / concentration along with proficiency of usage of the mirror increases, move onto larger objects like cars, houses, boats, planes etc. I am sure you are going to be skeptical whether you will really receive what you have willed the mirror to bring to reality. Remember, there's absolutely nothing that you cannot do / have if you correctly use the magick mirror. Believe.

Ok! Let us start!

1: Do the Qabalistic Cross.

2: After completion of the above exercise, sit comfortably on a chair, in front of a table, in a semi darkened room.

3: Do the relaxation exercise. After this, keep your eyes open during the operation.

4: First **clear the mirror** of any previous charges present on it.

5: Now proceed to charge the mirror with akashic fluid. As you do so, impregnate the fluid with the desire that it will manifest the material object very soon. If, for example, you wish to have the new Lamborghini sports car then you should be specific as to the model of the car, color, upholstery and other accessories. Visualize your dream car as strongly as possible while loading the akashic fluid in the mirror. Promise the akashic fluid that you will pay for the service. Do not break this promise.

6: Lock the charge in the mirror and program it that the akashic rays will flow out of the mirror to manifest your dream car in the driveway. Imagine that the car is actually standing there and believe that this car, which is in the akashic planes, will soon become a reality.

7: After that, mentally command the mirror that it will continuously charge itself and the akashic rays will flow from the mirror to the desired place in the driveway to manifest your car.

8: Keep the mirror in a safe place and ensure that it is not moved or touched until the desired result occurs. Otherwise, there will be a break in the proceedings and you will have to start all over again.

9: After your wish is granted, proceed to clear the mirror of any charges and wrap it in a silk cloth. Keep it in a safe place.

Do not think about the possible and the impossible. If you strongly believe in the immense creative powers of the akashic fluid, you will get your car in a mysterious fashion…..you might win the lottery…..you might receive a windfall or an inheritance…. the possibilities of receiving or buying the car are endless. Just be open to the opportunities coming your way.

You can do this exercise for any other material object of your desire. It is bound to manifest, if you have conducted the process correctly with a positive state of mind. It is the law of the universe to give you what you strongly desire and the akashic fluid is its medium.

Just remember that you cannot re-use this mirror until it has manifested the object of your desire or until you have cancelled the wish or cleared the mirror of previous charging.

It is preferable that you have more than one mirror constructed to carry out multiple operations at the same time. After the objective has been achieved, please remember to clear the mirror of the previous influences (see previous chapter).

II: How to use the magick mirror to attract money in your life?

1: Do the Qabalistic Cross.

2: After completion of the above exercise, sit comfortably on a chair, in front of a table, in a semi darkened room.

3: Do the relaxation exercise. After this, keep your eyes open during the operation.

4: First clear the mirror of any previous charges present on it.

5: Now proceed to charge the mirror with akashic fluid. As you do so, impregnate the fluid with the desire that it will manifest lots of money (specify the amount) very soon. Visualize this as strongly as possible while loading the akashic fluid in the mirror. Promise the akashic fluid that you will pay for the service. Do not break this promise.

6: Lock the charge in the mirror and program it that the akashic rays will flow out of the mirror to fill your room with money.

7: Visualize the rays flowing out of the mirror bringing tons of money and filling the room with the cash. Experience this abundance. Feel that you have more money than you could ever spend or ask for. Experience the feelings of joy, security, and excitement this money brings you.

8: After that, mentally command the mirror that it will continuously charge itself and the akashic rays will flow from the mirror and bring tons of money in your life.

9: Keep the mirror in a safe place and ensure that it is not moved or touched until the desired result occurs.

Otherwise, there will be a break in the proceedings and you will have to start all over again.

III: How to use the magick mirror to attract the person of your dreams?

At the outset, let me warn you that it is wrong to use magick to force a specific person to love you. What if that person has no feelings for you, hates you, is in love or married to someone else? It is volition of free will. Yes! It is quite possible to bring such a person in your life but the end result will not bring you happiness. That person was not for you in the first place at all. Always focus on the qualities you want in your mate. So, don't be vague. Suppose you want a nerdy but highly sexed girlfriend who loves to travel, then, tell the akashic fluid about it.

After making this wish, don't hanker for instant results. If you become impatient and begin to date someone else and this person begins to occupy your personal space, you are surely going to overlook the person you had wished for. You might not be able to recognize your soul mate, when that person appears before you, because you were so busy with your current date. The person of your dreams will walk away even before you know he / she was there. Be patient. Allow the akashic fluid / universe to fulfill your wish.

Try out the following method to attract the person of your dreams:

1: Do the Qabalistic Cross.

2: After completion of the above exercise, sit comfortably on a chair, in front of a table, in a semi darkened room.

3: Do the relaxation exercise. After this, keep your eyes open during the operation.

4: First clear the mirror of any previous charges present on it.

5: Now proceed to charge the mirror with akashic fluid. As you do so, impregnate the fluid with the desire that it will manifest the person of your dreams. Specify the gender, age-group, qualities and physical characteristics of the person you would like to have in your life. (Be practical with your expectations).

6: Visualize this as strongly as possible while loading the akashic fluid in the mirror.

7: Lock the charge in the mirror and programme it that the akashic rays will flow out of the mirror to bring you the person of your dreams. Promise the akashic fluid that you will pay for the service. Do not break this promise.

8: Keep the mirror in a safe place and ensure that it is not moved or touched until the desired result occurs. Otherwise, there will be a break in the proceedings and you will have to start all over again.

Be positive and have faith in the powers of the akashic fluid. Miraculously the person of your dreams will appear in your life.

IV: How to use the magick mirror for healing?

Please note that the magick mirror is not a substitute for medical treatment or surgical procedure for the patient's ailments. Use the mirror in conjunction with your doctor's treatment to hasten recovery or to prevent a sickness reaching the stage where a surgical procedure becomes necessary. At every stage, while using the magick mirror, the medical treatment is to be simultaneously continued until the patient is cured.

There are two methods of psychic healing using the magical mirror-

A: The first method involves filling the room, where the patient is kept, with the akashic rays so that the patient's whole body is bathed in them.

OR

B: The second direct method involves the akashic rays flowing to the patient's body. In this method the patient can be hundreds of miles away. No problem.

In the first method you should do the mirror operation in the room where the patient is lying.

1: Place the mirror on a table or the floor and proceed to charge, lock and programme the mirror as described previously.

2: While charging the mirror with the akashic fluid, impregnate it with the desire that it will cure the illness of the patient lying in the room. Promise the akashic fluid that you will pay for the service. Do not break this promise.

3: Then load the charge into the mirror and program the fluid to release and charge itself over the period of treatment.

4: The mirror should be kept in the room in a place where the rays emitted by it fills the entire room but ensure that the mirror will not be touched by others while It is in use.

In the second method,

1: The same procedure of charging, loading and programming the mirror is to be followed.

2: During charging, you must impregnate the akashic fluid with the desire that it will flow to the patient and make the sickness disappear. Distance is not a barrier. The patient can be hundreds of miles away from you. The akashic fluids are not bound by space or distance. No problem.

3: Now load the charge into the mirror and program the fluid to release and charge itself over the period of treatment. Promise the akashic fluid that you will pay for the service. Do not break this promise.

4: You will get better results if you can visualize the person, for whom the healing is intended, on the surface of the mirror or you may place a photograph or a lock of hair on the mirror during the loading process.

The patient will respond to medical treatment and recover miraculously!

V: How to visit people or places, in the astral body, using the magick mirror?

This exercise will require lots of practice and patience before you become proficient in it. A lack of self-esteem could prove to be a barrier to achieving the gift of vision. Be positive and patient. Do not be discouraged if you are unable to see anything in the initial stages. You will be able to get good results after constant practice.

1: Do the Qabalistic Cross and the Circuit of Light Exercise.

2: After completion of the above exercise, sit comfortably on a chair, in front of a table, in a semi darkened room.

3: Do the relaxation exercise. After this, keep your eyes open during the operation.

4: First clear the mirror of any previous charges present on it.

5: Now proceed to charge the mirror with akashic fluid. As you do so, impregnate the fluid with the desire that you wish to see the person or place. Visualize this as strongly as possible while loading the akashic fluid in the mirror.

6: Lock the charge in the mirror and program it that the akashic rays will flow out of the mirror to bathe you in it. Visualize the rays flowing out of the mirror and taking you to the person or the place you would want to visit, in your astral body. Promise the akashic fluid that you will pay for the service. Do not break this promise.

7: Initially, you will get hazy impressions of your subject but with practice you will be pulled into the mirror and directly to the person or place you visualized.

8: You can use this method to visit the planets and distant galaxies.

9: After completing the exercise, proceed to clear the mirror of any charges and wrap it in a silk cloth. Keep it in a safe place.

VI: How to use the magick mirror to time travel?

Since the akashic fluid is both timeless and space less, it is ideal for time travelling. This exercise will also require lots of practice and patience before you become proficient in it.

1: Do the Qabalistic Cross and the Circuit of Light Exercise.

2: After completion of the above exercise, sit comfortably on a chair, in front of a table, in a semi darkened room.

3: Do the relaxation exercise. After this, keep your eyes open during the operation.

4: First clear the mirror of any previous charges present on it.

5: Now, proceed to charge the mirror with the akashic fluid. As you do so, impregnate the fluid with the desire that you wish to go to a particular place at a specific date either in the past or future. Visualize this as strongly as possible while loading the akashic fluid in the mirror.

6: Lock the charge in the mirror and program it that the akashic rays will flow out of the mirror to bathe you in it. Visualize the rays flowing out of the mirror and taking you to the particular time-period desired by you. Promise the akashic fluid that you will pay for the service. Do not break this promise.

7: Initially, you will get hazy impressions but with practice you will start getting clearer images. How exciting would it be to go to the past to check historical facts or go to the future to check stock-market prices, lottery draws and games of chance?

8: Keep a note book of your visits to verify their accuracy. If you keep notes, then re-read the notes weeks or months later and you will be amazed at how accurate many of these visions were.

9: After completing the exercise, proceed to clear the mirror of any charges and wrap it in a silk cloth. Keep it in a safe place.

Here' the kicker: the future remains as a range of possibilities with a "most probable" scenario based on what holds the greatest energy. Even a 100% accurate vision of the most likely outcome will raise self doubts about whether you want that scenario to manifest. Your self-doubts can influence the outcome and make the original prediction look inaccurate. Also, some of the future visions could be what has / will take place in a parallel universe and not relevant to our plane of existence (see VII).

VII: How to use the magick mirror to visit your parallel / alternate self in a parallel universe?

According to multiverse theory, there are many worlds or universes alongside ours. Some of these universes, in terms of physical laws, can be found next to ours and others 'further away' in the sense that they are ruled by other laws of nature. A multiverse may consists of many parallel universes. Our universe and our earth is part of only one of many parallel universes in a larger multiverse.

The theory further elaborates that all possibilities which can happen will happen in another quantum reality and that depending on our choices there are an infinite number of realities, though existing in another quantum reality. In simplified terms it means there would be alternate realities of ourselves in parallel worlds like our own where you would be living your life time in various periods of time. Suppose you are a young student in your present existence, you could be a middle aged doctor or a trader, or a convict....married, divorced, young or old in the other worlds! How exciting it would be to visit our other selves and get their advice or envision what would happen if we took a certain decision now.

This exercise will need lots of practice and patience before you become an expert.

1: Do the Qabalistic Cross and the Circuit of Light Exercise.

2: After completion of the above exercise, sit comfortably on a chair, in front of a table, in a semi darkened room.

3: Do the relaxation exercise. After this, keep your eyes open during the operation.

4: First clear the mirror of any previous charges present on it.

5: Now proceed to charge the mirror with akashic fluid. As you do so, impregnate the fluid with the desire that you wish to visit your parallel self. Concentrate while loading the akashic fluid in the mirror.

6: Lock the charge in the mirror and programme it that the akashic rays will flow out of the mirror to bathe you in it. Visualize the rays flowing out of the mirror and taking you to the particular alternate self desired by you. Promise the akashic fluid that you will pay for the service. Do not break this promise.

7: Suppose you need to take a major decision about something: like getting a job in a particular industry; getting married or divorced; moving house; to have or not to have surgery etc. Charge the magick mirror to take you to your parallel self who has already taken the action for any of the above decisions. Check out his condition. Is he happy? Is he sad? You can talk to your other self in that parallel world and figure out what to do in the present.

You can also visit your other future possible selves who are more successful than you to help you figure something in the present. They will show you what you will achieve should you take that particular path. Anticipations in the present are messages sent to you from your future possible selves. Or you can think of another parallel where you are very rich or sexually active or powerful or athletic and you would like to be that person.

While charging the mirror with akashic fluid impregnate it with your wish to visit the parallel world where your other successful self resides and command the akashic fluid to draw the characteristics of that person in you. Feel the fullness of your success from that other parallel self, and assimilate it within you.

8: Remember that your parallels / alternative selves exist wherever you think they are. Everything is connected.

All experience and events are connected, in all times and places. You are connected to your thousands of alternate selves, and they are connected to you here.

9: After completing the exercise, proceed to clear the mirror of any charges and wrap it in a silk cloth. Keep it in a safe place.

VIII: How to use the magick mirror for exorcising 'possessed people' or 'haunted places'?

I would like to caution you that this operation is dangerous and should be carried out by experts only. So, if you are not experienced in the art of exorcism, then please do not attempt this operation.

If you wish to exorcise people who have been possessed by entities then-

1: Do the Qabalistic Cross and the Circuit of Light exercise. Fill the room with the pure white light emanating from you. This will help to cleanse the room and drive out evil influences.

2: Seat the afflicted person in front of the mirror which has been charged with the akashic fluid and impregnated with the desire that it will draw out the entity from the afflicted person's body. Promise the akashic fluid that you will pay for the service. Do not break this promise.

3: The charge is locked and programmed to flow and get continuously recharged till the entity is sucked by the akashic fluid into the depths of the mirror.

4: After the akashic fluid has absorbed the entity into the astral planes, request the akashic fluid to close the doorway connecting our world. This will prevent the banished entity from returning to this plane and cause troubles here.

5: Trace the banishing pentagram (see **Appendix #1**) over the mirror and also in the four directions of the room where the exorcism took place. The pentagram will drive away any evil influences present in the surroundings.

6: After completing the exercise, proceed to clear the mirror of any charges and wrap in a silk cloth. Keep it in a safe place.

7: Do the Qabalistic Cross once again for your protection.

8: You can also exorcise a haunted place in the same manner as above.

SO THERE YOU ARE! YOU ARE NOW PRIVY TO SOME GREAT MAGICKAL SECRETS. USE THEM WISELY AND SAFELY AND YOU WILL BENEFIT IMMENSELY FROM THE RESULTS.

APPENDIX

1: Tracing a Banishing Pentagram

A pentagram is a five pointed star. It serves as a psychic barrier to ward off evil forces confronting you. If you are accosted by an evil force then you should trace this pentagram in the direction of this force and chant the Holy Names of the Lord. This will prevent that force from attacking you. You can also trace this pentagram on the inside of the doors and windows of your house to keep away evil and bad luck.

1. To trace the pentagram, keep your left hand at your side.

2. Make a fist of your right hand and point with the extended forefinger.

3. Point outside your left hip / thigh. Trace with your extended finger an imaginary line up above your head, and then move your finger to the outside of your left hip / thigh.

4. Next, move your finger so that it is outside your left shoulder then horizontally across so that it is outside your right shoulder.

5. Finally, move it back to your left hip/ thigh, ending exactly where you started.

The figure of the pentagram should be drawn in front of you without breaks in between. Your forefinger should always be pointing forward away from you. Try to visualize the pentagram as a bright light while tracing its outline in front of you. Maintain this vision for as long as possible.

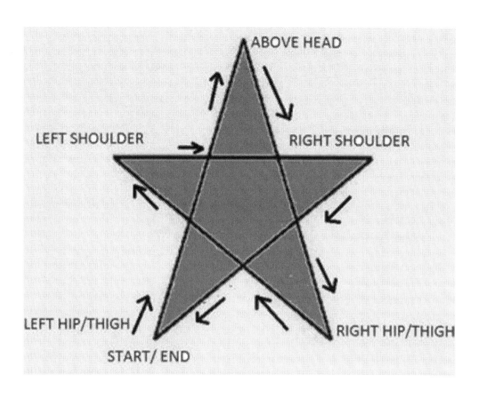

2: Planetary plants for organic fluid collector

To make an organic fluid collector, choose one or more than one plant from each planet category, in equal quantities (weight wise). Cut these plants into little pieces. Add a little water to the cut pieces and grind them to form a smooth paste. Now, add a suitable preservative to the paste and mix well. You may also add 2 teaspoons of powdered quartz to this mixture. Voila!

SUN

Angelica, balsam, corn, cinnamon, cardamom, common cabbage, chrysanthemum, clove tree, heliotrope, lavender, lotus, laurel, saffron, sage, thyme, red sandalwood, barley, orange tree.

MOON

Hay, camphor, cucumber, poppy, pumpkin, gourd, lettuce, melon, water-melon, beetroot, white sandalwood and lime-tree.

MARS

Absinthe, garlic, artichoke, asparagus, basil, belladonna, thistle, bean, mustard, onion, nutmeg, rhubarb and vine.

MERCURY

Acacia, aniseed, chicory, honeysuckle, wild rose, millet, marshmallow, hazelnut, tea, clover and juniper.

JUPITER

Aloe, amaranth, daisy, cedar, cherry tree, red cabbage, white fig tree, strawberry, mulberry, elm tree, poplar, peony, plum tree, sesame and violet.

VENUS

Almond tree, cassia, honey suckle, lemon tree, coriander, spinach, clover, mistletoe, iris, hyacinth, lily, rose, daisy and plantain.

SATURN

Cactus, hemlock, cocoa, cypress, datura, moss, fennel, lichen, black fig, male fern and tobacco plant.

Thank You!

Thanks for buying my book. Did you love it? If you enjoyed the book, please spread the word and leave a review on Amazon. Your opinion matters to me. Word-of-mouth publicity is crucial for any author to succeed. I would appreciate just a sentence or two.

Here's the Amazon link to my book-

http://www.amazon.com/dp/B00955LLF4
OR
 http://ASIN.cc/RahVJf

Please visit my Amazon Author Page
http://Author.to/MikeNach

Thanks again for your support!

MY OTHER BOOKS!

If you liked this book, you will like these too:

HOW TO BE THE MASTER OF THE UNIVERSE
http://ASIN.cc/ychKfq
https://www.createspace.com /5034839

Game of Illusions
http://ASIN.cc/ytWryA
https://www.createspace.com /5042255

Game of Life
http://ASIN.cc/1Q7_D9W
https://www.createspace.com/5344252

HOW TO GET ANYTHING YOU WANT? MAKE A MAGICK MIRROR!
http://ASIN.cc/RahVJf
https://www.createspace.com/5040665

How to Be Enriched in Every Way
http://ASIN.cc/12Jo4zL
https://www.createspace.com /5065824

THE 40 PARABLES OF INVESTING
http://ASIN.cc/11ujpiL
https://www.createspace.com /5029013

I CHING OF THE STOCK MARKET
http://ASIN.cc/bxxqcL
https://www.createspace.com /5069717

THE HARE AND THE TORTOISE -BEAT THE BULLIES!
http://ASIN.cc/mocBz0

The Little Book That Beats the Bullies
http://ASIN.cc/12QD6kW
https://www.createspace.com /5043967

DATING ADVICE: 30 Frequently Asked Questions
http://ASIN.cc/V_YBvf

WHY ME?
http://ASIN.cc/e5qS5f

Made in the USA
Lexington, KY
30 March 2015